COMPUTER INVESTIGATION

SOLVING CRIMES WITH SCIENCE:
Forensics

Computer Investigation

Criminal Psychology & Personality Profiling

DNA Analysis

Document Analysis

Entomology & Palynology

Explosives & Arson Investigation

Fingerprints, Bite Marks, Ear Prints

Forensic Anthropology

Forensics in American Culture

Mark & Trace Analysis

Pathology

Solving Crimes With Physics

COMPUTER INVESTIGATION

Elizabeth Bauchner

Mason Crest

Mason Crest
450 Parkway Drive, Suite D
Broomall, PA 19008
www.masoncrest.com

Printed and bound in the United States of America.

First printing
9 8 7 6 5 4 3 2 1

Series ISBN: 978-1-4222-2861-6
ISBN: 978-1-4222-2862-3
ebook ISBN: 978-1-4222-8948-8

The Library of Congress has cataloged the
hardcopy format(s) as follows:

Library of Congress Cataloging-in-Publication Data

Bauchner, Elizabeth.
  Computer investigation / Elizabeth Bauchner.
      p. cm. — (Solving crimes with science, forensics)
  Audience: 012.
  Audience: Grades 7 to 8.
  Includes index.
  ISBN 978-1-4222-2862-3 (hardcover) — ISBN 978-1-4222-2861-6 (series) — ISBN 978-1-4222-8948-8 (ebook)
  1. Computer crimes—Investigation—Juvenile literature. 2. Computer crimes—Juvenile literature. 3. Forensic sciences—Juvenile literature. I. Title.
  HV8079.C65B38 2014
  363.25'968—dc23
                                    2013006931

Produced by Vestal Creative Services.
www.vestalcreative.com

Contents

Introduction   6

1. Computer Investigations: An Overview   9

2. Hacking: Criminal and Ethical Implications   25

3. Spreading Digital Disease: Viruses, Worms,
     and Trojan Horses   45

4. Internet Scams   55

5. Corporate Fraud and Computer Evidence   69

6. "Traditional" Crimes Solved with Computer Forensics   83

7. Careers in Computer Forensics   97

Glossary   107

Further Reading   108

For More Information   109

Index   110

Picture Credits   111

Biographies   112

Introduction

By Jay A. Siegel, Ph.D.
Director, Forensic and Investigative Sciences Program
Indiana University, Purdue University, Indianapolis

It seems like every day the news brings forth another story about crime in the United States. Although the crime rate has been slowly decreasing over the past few years (due perhaps in part to the aging of the population), crime continues to be a very serious problem. Increasingly, the stories we read that involve crimes also mention the role that forensic science plays in solving serious crimes. Sensational crimes provide real examples of the power of forensic science. In recent years there has been an explosion of books, movies, and TV shows devoted to forensic science and crime investigation. The wondrously successful *CSI* TV shows have spawned a major increase in awareness of and interest in forensic science as a tool for solving crimes. *CSI* even has its own syndrome: the *"CSI* Effect," wherein jurors in real cases expect to hear testimony about science such as fingerprints, DNA, and blood spatter because they saw it on TV.

The unprecedented rise in the public's interest in forensic science has fueled demands by students and parents for more educational programs that teach the applications of science to crime. This started in colleges and universities but has filtered down to high schools and middle schools. Even elementary school students now learn how science is used in the criminal justice system. Most educators agree that this developing interest in forensic science is a good thing. It has provided an excellent opportunity to teach students science—and they have fun learning it! Forensic science is an ideal vehicle for teaching science for several reasons. It is truly multidisciplinary; practically every field of science has forensic applications. Successful forensic scientists must be good problem solvers and critical thinkers. These are critical skills that all students need to develop.

In all of this rush to implement forensic science courses in secondary schools throughout North America, the development of grade-appropriate resources that help guide students and teachers is seriously lacking. This new series: *Solving Crimes With Science: Forensics* is important and timely. Each book in the series contains a concise, age-appropriate discussion of one or more areas of forensic science.

Students are never too young to begin to learn the principles and applications of science. Forensic science provides an interesting and informative way to introduce scientific concepts in a way that grabs and holds the students' attention. *Solving Crimes With Science: Forensics* promises to be an important resource in teaching forensic science to students twelve to eighteen years old.

Computer Investigations: An Overview

In the 1990s, Bill Gates, the chief executive officer (CEO) of Microsoft Corporation, became a leading symbol of the computer industry. During this period, Microsoft was also accused of violating antitrust legislation, meaning they were suspected of using illegal business practices to **monopolize** the computer market and keep out competitors.

The biggest lawsuit alleged that Microsoft used illegal tactics to ensure that Internet Explorer, one of its products, became the public's exclusive "choice" for viewing Internet content. Bill Gates and Microsoft denied the charges. However, the investigators in the case searched large numbers of e-mails stored on Microsoft's computers and discovered evidence that the company had, in fact, attempted to oust competitors of Internet Explorer. The e-mails directly contradicted the claims of several Microsoft key executives.

In February 2000, Microsoft was found guilty of violating antitrust laws. The court concluded that Microsoft "maintained its monopoly power" by using "anticompetitive means" and "attempted to monopolize the Web browser market."

This case, like many crimes committed in today's world, was cracked open by investigators accessing e-mails and other files found on the suspects' computers. After obtaining the appropriate search warrants for the case, investigators were able to examine the files and programs of the suspect Microsoft computers to discover illegal activities. Through what's known as computer forensics, the investigators tracked down criminal evidence through recovery of lost, hidden, and deleted computer files.

Computer Crime, Computer Investigations

The digital age we entered at the end of the twentieth century has rapidly become an age of digital crime. Computer forensics deals with searching computers for evidence of crimes committed solely through the use of computers, known as cybercrime, and for evidence in "traditional" crimes—such as **corporate fraud** or homicide—that might be found on a computer. Examples of cybercrime include hacking, releasing computer viruses over the Internet, and various Internet scams such as selling phony merchandise or "spoofing" real websites.

The people who uncover digital evidence of criminal activity and help bring the perpetrators to justice are called computer forensic specialists or computer forensic technicians. A computer forensic specialist is an expert in finding lost, hidden, or deleted information on a computer. These specialists may work for the government, in law enforcement, or in private practice.

Computer forensics is basically a twofold process that includes many complex steps. The first part of the process is the investigation of computer data to find evidence of criminal activity. The second part of the process involves using the evidence found in the computer to help settle a dispute, either in or out of court.

According to John R. Vacca in Computer Forensics, many types of *civil* and criminal proceedings make use of computer forensic evidence. People who hire computer forensic specialists include:

- criminal prosecutors, who use computer evidence in a variety of cases where incriminating documents and files can be found, such as homicides, financial fraud, drug crimes, embezzlement, and child pornography
- law enforcement officials, who frequently require assistance from computer forensic specialists in the handling of seized computer equipment
- insurance companies, who may use computer evidence in false accident, arson, and workman's compensation claims
- corporations, who often hire forensics specialists to search employee computers for signs of sexual harassment, embezzlement, and theft of trade secrets or other internal or confidential information
- employees, who sometimes hire computer forensics specialists to support their claims of *wrongful termination*, sexual harassment, or age discrimination
- individuals involved in civil litigations (disputes between individual people as opposed to disputes between the state and an individual) can make use of personal and business records found on a computer in cases of fraud, divorce, discrimination, or harassment.

Computer Investigations: An Overview 11

Computer Forensics Versus Other Forensic Sciences

Computer forensics is quite different from other forensic science disciplines, such as DNA analysis or the study of **latent fingerprints**. Other forensic disciplines involve the study and application of science to the purposes of the law. Through scientific analysis and evaluation of certain data, such as hair or fibers found at the crime scene, forensic scientists can often determine, with a high level of probability, who was at the scene of a crime or who committed it.

For example, let's say investigators discover blood at the scene of a crime. Through DNA analysis, forensic scientists develop specific identifying in-

Computer forensic specialists may be called on to investigate wrongful termination claims.

formation relative to an individual, and then conclude that the individual was at the crime scene. To support their conclusions, they gather extensive statistical data on the DNA profiles from which they base their conclusions.

Computer forensic specialists, on the other hand, don't normally attempt to make interpretive or evaluative comments on the data they discover. In most cases, they do not make scientific judgments about the data. Rather, they extract or produce computer data that stands on its own, such as the e-mails in the Microsoft antitrust case. In their investigations, they look for the information relevant to the case, such as accounting ledgers in an embezzlement case or incriminating photographs or e-mails in a child pornography case. Like all forensic scientists, they treat their evidence as though it will be presented in court, but they do not ordinarily attempt to interpret the information using scientific methods.

Computer Forensic Specialists Must Be Professional

Since a computer contains a vast amount of data, a computer forensic specialist will sometimes come across data that is not relevant to the case and is legally protected under client privacy laws. For example, a computer forensic specialist investigating a physician accused of harassment may very well come across client records that have nothing to do with the case. When information about uninvolved people is inadvertently accessed, it is the legal and ethical responsibility of the computer forensic specialist not to divulge this client information.

In addition to being an impartial investigator, a computer forensic specialist will typically have a wide range of experience with various types of computer hardware and software programs. The computer forensic special-

ist must be able to search a computer thoroughly enough to access deleted files, encrypted files, password-protected files, and other forms of hidden evidence. Additionally, the specialist should know where on the computer to look for the most relevant data in the case.

Computer forensic specialists can perform either on-site inspections of the computer or laboratory inspections on seized computer equipment. Either way, they first must copy all the files from the computer. This is a very important step, because if specialists do it wrong or alter data in any way, the evidence may not be admissible in court. To ensure that nothing about the data is changed, destroyed, or altered, they do not turn on the suspect computer but instead use special technology to make a backup—or mirrored—copy of the suspect computer hard drive. A backup copy contains the same material as the original, and the computer forensic specialists can then search the mirrored copy for evidence without accidentally destroying any of the original evidence.

By following an established set of rules for collecting computer evidence, computer forensic specialists can ensure that all evidence is protected. According to Vacca, a knowledgeable computer forensic specialist will carefully handle a computer system to ensure that:

- No possible evidence is damaged, destroyed, or otherwise compromised by the procedures used to investigate the computer.
- No computer viruses or worms are introduced during the analysis.
- All extracted and possibly relevant evidence is properly handled.
- The evidence obtained stays within a set chain of custody, meaning only designated investigators have access to the evidence.
- Business operations of the computer forensic client are affected for only a short amount of time, if at all.
- Any privileged client information inadvertently acquired during the search is ethically and legally respected and not divulged.

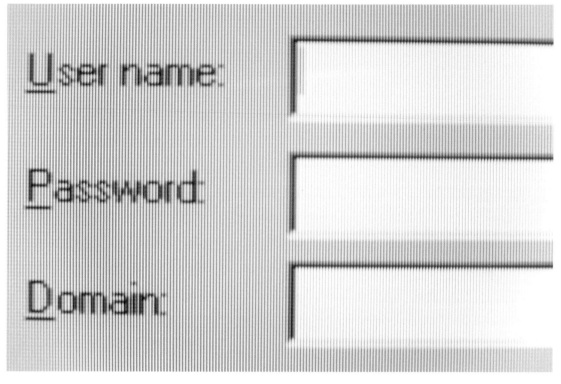

Password-protected files are one obstacle computer forensic specialists must overcome.

Steps Taken by
Computer Forensic Specialists

In order to identify and retrieve possible evidence from a computer system, Vacca explains in Computer Forensics that computer forensic specialists must take several careful steps:

- Protect the computer system during the forensic investigation from any possible alteration, damage, data corruption, or virus introduction.

How Computers Work

Computers are very powerful tools that contain billions of bits (which stands for BinarydigITs) of information—the tiniest pieces of computer data. In order for us to accomplish tasks on a computer, we need a combination of hardware, software, and input.

Hardware consists of devices like the computer itself—the monitor, keyboard, printer, mouse, and speakers. Inside the container where we turn the computer on is the hard drive, otherwise known as the hard disk, along with more pieces of hardware, including the central processing unit (CPU). The CPU contains the main processing chips, tiny wafers of silicon that contain miniature electric circuits that store millions of bits of information. The hardware processes the commands it receives from the software and performs the tasks and calculations the software requires.

Software is the name given to all the programs that can be installed on a computer to perform certain activities. Most important is the operating system software, such as Windows for a PC or OSX for Apple computers. The operating system manages all the hardware and software resources of the computer system. Then there is application software, such as Microsoft Word for creating documents.

Input is provided by the computer user. When you type a command or click on an icon, you are telling the computer what to do and providing input. The first input you provide is when you turn on the computer, or boot the system. The operating system software tells the CPU to start certain programs and to turn on some hardware devices so they are ready for more input from you.

Even deleted files can be recovered by a computer forensic specialist.

- Discover all files on the computer, including existing normal files, deleted yet remaining files, hidden files, password-protected files, and encrypted files.
- Recover all or as much as possible of discovered deleted files.
- Reveal to the extent possible the contents of hidden files as well as temporary or swap files used by both the application software programs and the operating system software.

Computer Investigations: An Overview   17

- Access the contents of protected and encrypted files to the extent that is necessary, possible, and legal.
- Analyze all possibly relevant data found in special and typically inaccessible areas of the computer disk.
- Print out an overall analysis of the subject computer system, as well as a listing of all possibly relevant files and discovered file data.
- Provide an opinion of the system layout; the file structures discovered; any discovered data and authorship information; and any attempts to hide, delete, protect, or encrypt information.
- Provide expert consultation and testimony, as needed.

How Data Can Be Hidden on a Computer

Data is stored on the computer disk in the form of files. A file is simply a named collection of bytes (each byte equals eight bits). The bytes might be the instructions of a software application or the records of a database, or they could be the pixel colors for a GIF image. No matter what it contains, a file is simply a string of bytes. When a program running on the computer requests a file, the hard disk retrieves its bytes and sends them to the CPU one at a time.

The computer hard drive consists of mirror-smooth disks, called platters, which are made of aluminum or glass. They have the ability to store millions of bits of information. A tiny motor spins the platters extremely fast. Another tiny instrument, called an arm, moves over the platters from the center outward and back, extracts the stored bits of information, and sends it on to the CPU for processing. In general, the arm moves back and forth over the plat-

Fast Fact

A typical desktop computer has a hard disk capacity of between 60 gigabytes and 3 terabytes. One terabyte is 1,024 gigabytes, and one gigabyte is 1,024 megabytes. Bytes are a combination of eight bits to represent one character of data. And bits? Bits are the smallest piece of computer data, represented by a 1 or 0. Bit is short for "binary digit," which is the "language" of computers.

ters at a rate of about fifty times per second. The more platters inside a hard drive, the more information the computer can hold.

Data is stored on the surface of a platter in sectors and tracks. Tracks are *concentric* circles around the platter, and sectors are pie-shaped wedges on a track. Each sector contains a fixed number of bytes in which information can be stored. For example, many computer platter sectors can store either 256 or 512 bytes.

Typically, there are unused spaces on the disks that can become repositories of information that people are attempting to hide. For example, a file's slack space is the remnant area at the end of a file. There is also unallocated space on a disk: space that is freed when someone deletes a file. However, just hitting the delete button only removes it from the user's view; it doesn't actually remove the file from the hard drive until the computer fills that space again with new data. Usually it takes months or even years before the computer uses that space again, so in most cases, deleted files can be easily accessed by computer forensic specialists.

Computer forensic specialists must be familiar with both computer hardware and software.

Narrowing the Search: Why Examiners Cannot Search Every File

With personal computer systems currently reaching the capacity to store a hundred gigabytes of information, it is highly impractical for computer forensic specialists to search an entire computer for information. Furthermore, there may be legal prohibitions against searching every file, such as the client privacy rights mentioned earlier.

The biggest roadblock, however, is not the impracticality of scanning every file on a computer system, but the sheer physical difficulty for law enforcement personnel to read and assimilate the vast amounts of information contained in the files. For example, just twelve gigabytes of printed text would create a stack of paper twenty-four stories high! So for strictly practical reasons, computer forensic specialists cannot possibly search, print, and read every file.

Even when forensic specialists may have the legal right to search every file on the computer, time limitations often will not permit it. So how do computer forensic specialists get their jobs done? They get the best results when they have as many details of the case as possible. With the right details, computer forensic specialists can create a list of search terms in order to find specific and case-related information from a large group of files.

Computer Forensic Technology

As previously explained, computer forensics involves the preservation, identification, extraction, and documentation of computer evidence stored in the form of data (files). Often, the data was created transparently by the

The Internet introduces many opportunities for cybercrime.

computer's operating system and without the knowledge of the computer operator. Attempts to hide, delete, or corrupt files to cover crimes can often be discovered by competent computer forensic specialists because they have special tools and techniques that help them find and preserve the computer evidence.

Some of the tools available to computer forensic specialists enable them to identify passwords, log-ons, and other information that is automatically dumped from the computer memory. Other tools can be used to identify backdated files and to tie files to the computers that created them.

Most computer forensic technology is not available to the public. For example, TextSearchNT, a computer forensic software program, is widely used by government agencies, corporations, and law enforcement agencies throughout the world, but it is not available for purchase by individuals.

This powerful software program allows the computer to quickly search hard drives for key words or specific text patterns. It also quickly searches slack and unallocated file space.

Although the public may not have access to the tools used by professional computer forensic specialists, many of the problems caused by computer crimes, such as hacking, directly affect the public, and we can take steps to protect ourselves and our computers.

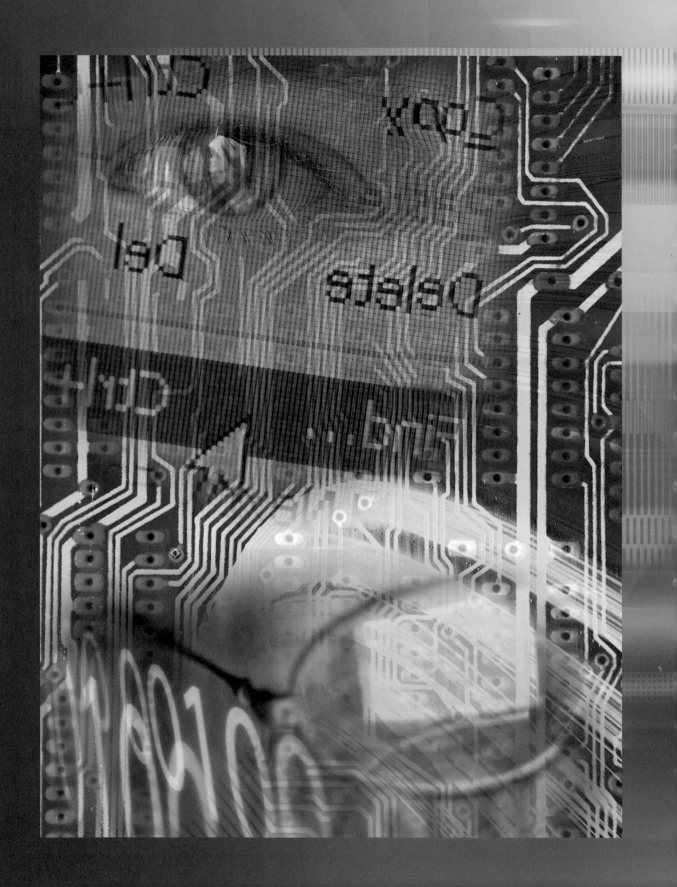

Hacking: Criminal and Ethical Implications

2

On February 7, 2000, one of the world's largest Internet sites, Yahoo!, was hit with a flood of data at speeds higher than one gigabit per second, the equivalent of more than 3.5 million average e-mail messages every minute. The initial flood of data overwhelmed one of Yahoo!'s main routers. The router recovered, but then Yahoo! lost all routing from one of its major Internet Service Providers (ISPs).

It didn't take long for Yahoo! system administrators to realize that the flood of data clogging their servers was not caused by a random glitch but by a deliberate attack on their system. In fact, it was a highly sophisticated attack that used many other computers as pawns to conduct the attack. One of the computers used in the attack even belonged to Yahoo! The attack, called a denial-of-service (DoS), was the largest attack to date, and experts believed it could only be the work of a very sophisticated hacker or group of hackers.

Later that evening, an FBI agent working undercover as a computer hacker went online to chat with other hackers on an Internet Relay Chat (IRC) board. The FBI agent used the **handle** Swallow, and that night was acting as the channel operator for an IRC chat room frequented by hackers. A hacker who called himself Mafiaboy came online and started bragging about a huge hack he had pulled off. No one in the chat room believed him, including the FBI agent, because Mafiaboy had been around before and often bragged about his "skilz" in an obnoxious and off-putting manner.

The next morning, Buy.com, an online retail store, issued its initial public offering of stock to investors. Things were going well for nearly two hours until the website became crippled under the load of a massive DoS attack. Later that afternoon, eBay reported significant outages of service, as did Amazon.com. In two days' time, the Internet business world, including **e-commerce** and online stock trading, had become threatened as a reliable method of conducting business by the largest hacker attacks to date.

Fast Fact

A denial-of-service (DoS) attack is one whose purpose isn't to break into a system, but to deny others' use of the system. A DoS attack may crash a system, disconnect two or more systems, slow down a system, or send a system into an infinite "loop," that is, a continual state of crashing and restarting until an administrator manually stops and restarts the machine.

Later that night, Swallow went online again, hoping to find some leads into what was happening in the online world. Once again, Mafiaboy came online and started bragging about how he had pulled off the hacks, and once again, nobody believed him. Mafiaboy was what is known as a "script-kiddie" in the hacking world, which simply means someone without a lot of experience or knowledge in hacking. No one in the IRC chat session thought a script-kiddie could pull off such a sophisticated series of attacks on some of the world's largest websites.

That's when Mafiaboy challenged the other hackers: "What do you want me to hit next?" he typed to the group. Someone suggested CNN.com and E*Trade. Within minutes, CNN's global network, including their news website and 1,200 other websites they hosted, began to grind to a halt under the heavy load of excessive traffic. By the following morning, E*Trade and Datek, online stock-trading companies, were dealing with sporadic Internet outages.

Chat room dialogue

Hacking: Criminal and Ethical Implications

How Internet Networks Work

Every computer that is connected to the Internet is part of a network. Some networks are small, some are very large. They all work together so that when you send an e-mail to anyone anywhere in the world, it arrives within seconds.

At school, you may be part of a local area network (LAN), where all the computers in the school are connected. The LAN then connects to the Internet using an ISP that your school has contracted with. When you connect with the ISP, you become part of their network. The ISP may then connect to a larger network and become part of their network. The Internet is simply a network of networks.

Large communications companies connect various geographical regions through what's called a Point of Presence (POP). The POP is where you'd connect locally to a larger network. The POPs of different companies then connect to each other through Network Access Points (NAPs). In this way, customers of different ISPs can have their computers communicate with each other.

The networks rely on NAPs, backbones, and routers to send data from computer to computer. Backbones are typically fiber optic cables combined together to increase their capacity to send data. Routers are specialized computers that determine where to send information from one computer to another; they make sure that information goes where it's supposed to, and ensure that information does not go where it is not needed.

Each and every computer on the Internet can be identified through its Internet Protocol (IP) address. IP is the language computers use to talk with each other. Other identifying means are a computer's domain name and Uniform Resource Locator (URL).

As the computer forensic evidence on the source of the attacks was pieced together, it became clear that dozens of computers from several universities in the United States and Canada had been hijacked for use in the attacks. The hacker had planted malicious software on the university computer systems that turned them into launching pads for massive DoS attacks.

Almost overnight, the public's trust in Internet business was nearly ruined. The press glommed onto the story as though it were the end of the world. And all that investigators knew at the time was that it might possibly be an obnoxious script-kiddie known online as Mafiaboy. They had to find him, and find him fast.

What Is a Hacker Anyway?

The term hacker is often used to describe a person who breaks into other people's computers to wreak havoc on their systems or to steal information, but this type of hacker is only a small fraction of the hacker population. The term actually dates back to the early 1960s at the engineering department at the Massachusetts Institute of Technology (MIT), where it was used to describe students with a mastery of computers who could push programs beyond what they were designed to do.

A hacker, therefore, is a person who enjoys exploring the details of programmable systems, such as computers and cell phones, and attempts

"Black hat" hackers commit malicious acts using their advanced understanding of computers.

DoS attacks can disrupt the flow of online business.

to understand the finer points of how to use them and stretch their capabilities. Hackers may specialize in certain areas of computing, such as computer programming or specific operating systems, or they may work for companies testing their security systems.

Hackers understand much more about computers than the typical user. They are not usually malicious meddlers like Mafiaboy, who use their computer skills to break into computer systems in order to slow down or interrupt business, or to steal information like credit card numbers. The correct term for that type of hacker is "cracker," though most people don't use the word.

"Ethical" hackers, the ones who use their skills to further their knowledge of computers or to put their knowledge to work for legitimate businesses,

Hacking: Criminal and Ethical Implications

are known as "white hat" hackers. "Black hat" hackers are the malicious individuals who give this term its bad reputation.

Hackers of all stripes are somewhat of an elite group of people on the Internet. They can be an extremely cooperative and yet very competitive group. Because hacking is so complicated and technical, hackers tend to admire and respect each other. A basic hacker ethic is that information should be made widely available and shared freely. However, you have to prove yourself a capable hacker before being accepted into the group. Hackers also have their own organizations, websites, contests, and conferences.

Computer Forensics in the Search for Mafiaboy

On February 12, a few days after the Yahoo! attack, Dell Computer Corporation reported that its systems had been hit with a massive DoS attack. Once again, Mafiaboy claimed responsibility for the attack. By this time, however, several hackers posing as Mafiaboy were also online claiming responsibility, as were other hackers going by different names. People who hadn't committed the hacks were even trying to turn themselves in to the FBI in an effort to gain respect and admiration in the hacker community.

Within a couple of days, however, the FBI was able to find a webpage for Mafiaboy. The website belonged to a user of Delphi Supernet in Canada. Shortly thereafter, forensic evidence linked the Dell attack to an Internet account with an ISP in Montreal called TOTALNET. The FBI now had two pieces of evidence pointing to a Mafiaboy in Canada, so they involved the Royal Canadian Mounted Police (RCMP) in their search. The RCMP and the FBI dubbed the investigation Operation Claymore.

The Trouble Black Hat Hackers Can Cause

Hackers like Mafiaboy can cause a lot of problems for businesses and individuals. In addition to administering DoS attacks, which cause delays and slow down Internet traffic, malicious hacks can be classified into three other categories: obtaining information, such as credit card numbers, to use or to sell; destruction of data, such as entire bank accounts; and alteration of data, such as grade changing.

In a worst-case scenario, acts of terrorism can be committed on-line through computer hacking, such as stealing secret government data or spying on government activities. Furthermore, online terrorist acts could be coordinated with real-time terrorist attacks. For example, a bomb could be planted in a building and set to go off at a specified time. At the same time, a computer hacker could break into the system of the fire and police departments to completely cut off rescue personnel communications to add to the confusion and terror.

The RCMP appointed agent Mark Gosselin to the case, who immediately executed a search warrant for the computer systems of Delphi Supernet and TOTALNET. Gosselin found three e-mail accounts registered to a Mafiaboy, and began a long and tedious process of pouring through the

Computer forensic specialists can trace an e-mail to the computer from which it came.

account information, cross-checking telephone and credit card numbers with names on the accounts and mailing addresses. Nothing matched up, except for one phone number.

Interestingly, this phone number was familiar to Gosselin, who, months before, investigated a hack into a high school computer system in Oregon that had been traced back to an account at Delphi Supernet. That investigation had gone nowhere, and Gosselin hadn't looked at the files in a long time. However, during the Mafiaboy investigation, when he performed a search for addresses against that phone number, he returned a match to the previous investigation: a home on Rue de Golf, outside Montreal.

Feeling he had a good, solid lead into the whereabouts of Mafiaboy, Gosselin obtained a search warrant to install dialed-number recorders (DNRs) on the telephone lines leading in and out of Mafiaboy's home. A DNR is the equivalent of a caller ID system that tracks all outgoing calls made from a suspect's telephone, with the difference being that in addition to telephone numbers called from the home, it detects all ISPs with which the suspect's computer connects. The drawback to DNRs is that they can't capture voices, only phone numbers and dates and times of calls.

Still, the DNR at Mafiaboy's residence helped investigators tremendously. For one thing, they learned about another TOTALNET account registered to Mafiaboy; however, this new account was registered to the company that Mafiaboy's father owned. Investigators soon learned that Mafiaboy had several methods for connecting to the Internet, and also had several legitimate e-mail accounts, hacked e-mail accounts, and e-mail accounts ostensibly belonging to family members. Investigators also discovered that three teenage men lived in the home with a father and a mother.

Although the RCMP had narrowed down the search to a single residence, the question remained: who was sitting at the computer when the attacks

Hacking: Criminal and Ethical Implications

35

Case Study:
Another Infamous Hacker

Kevin Mitnick is probably the most infamous hacker in the United States. As a teenager, he was a phone "phreaker" (a hacker term for phone hackers), making free long distance calls before Pacific Bell caught him. He was arrested and placed on probation.

In 1982, Mitnick received national attention when he hacked into the North American Aerospace Defense Command (NORAD). In the late 1980s, he took control of three central telephone offices in New York City, as well as all of the phone-switching centers in California. In 1989, he was charged with computer fraud and possession of unauthorized access devices that he used for hacking. He was sentenced to and served a year in jail.

In 1991, he violated probation by hacking into voicemail systems at Pacific Bell. After the government got a warrant for his arrest in 1992, Mitnick became a fugitive. During that time, he went on a national hacking spree that earned him a spot on the FBI's most wanted list. Over a two-and-a-half-year period, he hacked into computers, stole corporate secrets, scrambled phone networks, and broke into the national defense warning system.

Mitnick was finally found, not by the government, who he successfully eluded time and again, but by computer savant Tsutomu Shimomura, after Mitnick broke into Shimomura's home computer

network. At the time, Shimomura was a security specialist at the San Diego Supercomputer Center and had originally declined to assist authorities in finding Mitnick. But when Mitnick broke into Shimomura's system, he agreed to help find him.

Working with the FBI, Shimomura determined Mitnick was making telephone calls with a cellular modem to a Netcom phone bank in Raleigh, North Carolina. Shimomura and the investigative team were able to narrow the location to somewhere near the Raleigh-Durham International Airport. Mitnick had used his computer skills to make the phone number he was calling from untraceable, but investigators were able to track him down by using cellular frequency detection devices. How? Cell phones are equipped with an "electronic serial number" (ESN). Through special monitoring hardware, Shimomura and the investigators were able to track the transmission signal of the cell phone and determine the ESN "tag" of Mitnick's communications. Basically, the team drove around in the Raleigh area until they had a clear "fix." Mitnick was found and arrested in an apartment complex.

Mitnick eventually signed a plea agreement and was released from prison on January 21, 2001, after being incarcerated for five years. He was prohibited from using a computer and from acting as a consultant or adviser in computer-related matters until January 20, 2003. More recently, Mitnick has claimed to go "legit" and has written three books—two on hacking and computer security systems, and an autobiography.

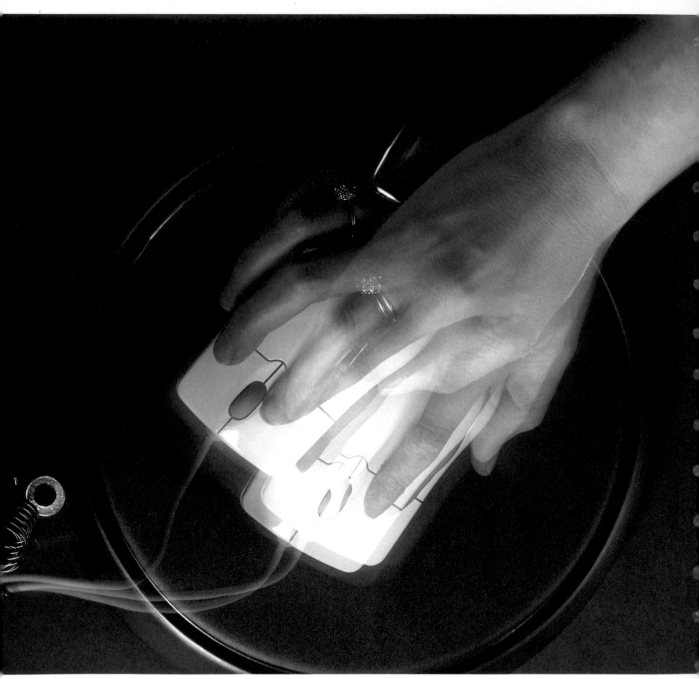

In the search for Mafiaboy, investigators had to monitor several different Internet accounts.

occurred? With the evidence collected so far, investigators were able to obtain a court order to intercept all private communications of Mafiaboy and his entire immediate family for sixty days. This included a **wiretap** and a massive data collection operation including all telephone conversations and computer and Internet activity that took place in the home.

For the next forty-three days, the RCMP and the FBI closely monitored Mafiaboy and his family's phone and computer communications. Data interceptors were also set up at the ISP where Mafiaboy had e-mail accounts. Every day, the data was captured and reconstructed using software created by the FBI. In this manner, the RCMP was able to sift through the massive amounts of data and look for clues that would help them build a case against Mafiaboy.

Mafiaboy's Activities and Arrest

Mafiaboy was actually not all that good at hacking. Most of the tools he used had been given to him by more experienced hackers or was software

he had downloaded from the Internet. The DoS tools he used in his attacks against Yahoo! and the other businesses included Stacheldraht (the German word for barbed wire) and a variant of a malicious software program called Tribal Flood Network (TFN) that swarms target systems and overloads them with data requests. Like most script-kiddies, he did not write the tools or the code for the programs himself.

A few weeks after the investigation into Mafiaboy's communications began, his father installed a digital subscriber line (DSL), which greatly increased the amount of data to be captured. Investigators continued to watch as Mafiaboy attempted new hacks and tried to learn new software. Most of his online activities, however, were Internet-gaming and chats in IRC until the wee hours of the morning.

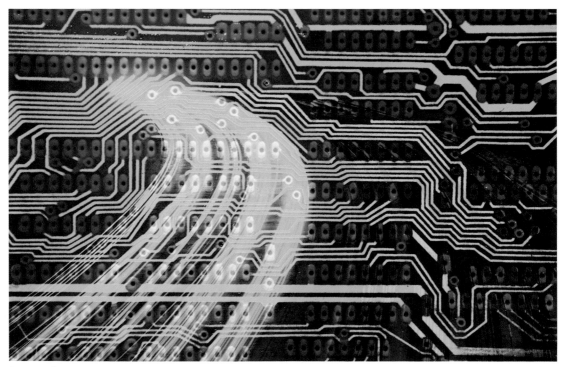

Investigators had to pour over a massive amount of data to pinpoint the location of Mafiaboy.

"Script-kiddies" often do not create the destructive programs they use to attack other computers. They use preexisting programs instead.

The key pieces of evidence linking Mafiaboy to the DoS attacks came from the wiretap. While the computer evidence pointed to someone in the residence committing the attacks, the wiretap pointed to which one of the brothers committed the hacks. Mafiaboy turned out to be the youngest of the three. He was fourteen years old at the time of the DoS attacks.

Gosselin had every intention of keeping the wiretap going for the full sixty days he was authorized to use it. However, just a month into the investigation they heard Mafiaboy's father make plans to hire a hit man to assault a business colleague over a dispute involving a $1.5 million transaction. On day forty-three of the investigation, after hearing the father on the telephone agree with another man that "tonight's the night," the RCMP

Hacking: Criminal and Ethical Implications   41

Computer forensic specialists will search through discarded computer hardware to uncover hidden clues.

raided the house at 3:00 in the morning. They couldn't wait any longer and risk someone being killed.

When they raided the house, Mafiaboy wasn't home. His father and stepmother said he was sleeping at a friend's house. When police arrived at the friend's house, they found Mafiaboy calmly waiting outside on the curb, fully dressed. He had thrown his hard drives into a nearby lake or river; he wouldn't say which one. Still, investigators had enough computer forensic evidence to arrest him, and he was later sentenced to eight months in a juvenile detention center. He was also prohibited from possessing any software not commercially available, banned from using the Internet to talk with other hackers, and banned from hacking into other websites. The judge also ordered Mafiaboy to tell authorities the name of his ISP.

While hackers can cause real problems for Internet businesses and government agencies, another form of hacking—releasing computer viruses and worms over the Internet—can cause definite damage to individuals' personal computers.

3

Spreading Digital Disease: Viruses, Worms, and Trojan Horses

In the summer of 2003, a Minnesota teenager named Jeffrey Lee Parson downloaded a copy of the MS Blaster Internet worm and modified it to make his own version. The original worm was designed to launch a DoS attack on a Microsoft website by directing infected computers to the site. However, Microsoft quickly became aware of the problem and took immediate steps to lessen the effects of the attack.

Parson's worm managed to cripple tens of thousands of computers. First, Parson used the worm to infect about fifty computers. From those fifty computers, the worm spread to hundreds of other computers, and within a couple of days it had infected more than 48,000 computers. Overall, the FBI believes Parson's worm infected over a million computers in the United States and Canada.

Parson's version of the worm also gave him secret access, through the Internet, to computers that were infected by the worm. After he was caught, Parson admitted that he created his worm by modifying the original MS Blaster worm and adding a mechanism that gave him complete access to certain infected computers, allowing him remote control over the other computers from his computer. The creator of the original MS Blaster worm has not been caught.

Worms, along with viruses and Trojan horses, are all malicious programs created by people who intend to cause damage to or wreak havoc on other people's computers. They can cause real damage like erasing a computer hard disk, or just send silly and annoying messages. They are often referred to interchangeably, but although they share certain similarities, they are quite different.

Viruses

A computer virus attaches itself to a program or file so that it can spread from one computer to another, leaving infections as it travels. These mini-programs are called viruses because they share some common traits with biological viruses. Computer viruses spread from computer to computer much like biological viruses spread from person to person.

A biological virus is a fragment of DNA inside a protective jacket. Unlike a cell, a virus cannot reproduce. Instead, it spreads by injecting its DNA into living cells. The viral DNA then uses the cell to reproduce itself and spread. A computer virus shares some of these traits. Neither computer viruses nor biological viruses can reproduce on their own; a computer virus must piggyback on top of some other program or document in order to spread. Once the infected program or file is opened or running, the

Fast Fact

Computer viruses can only be spread with the help of a person; they do not spread by themselves. People spread viruses unintentionally and often unknowingly by sharing infected files or e-mails with others.

virus will also start spreading. It is then able to infect other programs or documents.

Worms

A worm is similar to a virus in its design and is considered to be a subclass of a virus. It is a computer program that has the ability to copy itself from machine to machine, but unlike a virus, it has the ability to travel from computer to computer without any help from a person. Worms normally move around and infect other computers through networks. Using a network, a worm can expand from a single copy incredibly quickly, as happened with the Blaster worm.

The biggest danger with a worm is its ability to replicate itself on a computer system, so rather than one computer sending out one copy of a single worm, it could actually send out hundreds or even thousands of copies of itself. Due to the copying nature of a worm and its ability to spread rapidly across networks, the end result in many cases is that the worm consumes too much system memory, which can cause web servers, network servers, and individual computers to stop working properly. In the case of the

Case Study:
Code Red

Another worm that made huge headlines was the Code Red worm in 2001. In just nine hours, it managed to replicate itself over 250,000 times. Experts originally thought the worm to be so powerful that it could cause the Internet to completely grind to a halt.

Code Red did slow down Internet traffic when it began to replicate itself, but not nearly as completely as had been predicted. It spread through the Internet, searching for computers hooked up to networks using Microsoft NT or Windows 2000 servers. Each time it found a server that did not have a security patch installed, the worm copied itself to that server. The new copy then scanned the Internet for other servers to infect.

The Code Red worm was designed to do three things:

- replicate itself for the first twenty days of each month.
- replace webpages on infected servers with a page that declared "Hacked by Chinese."
- launch a DoS attack on the White House web server in an attempt to overwhelm it and thereby shut it down.

On successful infection, the worm would wait for the appointed hour and connect to the www.whitehouse.gov domain. The attack would consist of the infected systems simultaneously sending a hundred connections to one port of the White House domain.

The worm, however, was discovered by eEye Digital Security, who immediately reported it to the National Infrastructure Protection Center (NIPC). NIPC was able to take steps to prevent it from spreading and doing real damage to the White House Web servers.

Blaster worm, Parson specially designed it to tunnel into personal computer systems and allow other users to control these computers.

Trojan Horses

Trojan horses derive their name from the tricky, mythological wooden animal that deceived the citizens of Troy. Computer Trojans appear to be legitimate software programs or games for people to download off the Internet. Unlike viruses or worms, Trojans cannot replicate themselves automatically, nor can they infect other files. They are simply phony software applications that say they do one thing and then really do another.

Trojan horses can do a lot of damage, from erasing your hard disk to deleting files. Some Trojans are more silly and annoying than malicious, and simply perform tasks like rearranging your desktop or adding joke icons to your computer.

Preventing Viruses and Protecting Your Computer

By taking a few simple steps, we can all protect our computers from viruses. Microsoft operating systems are generally more vulnerable to the spread of worms and other viruses than other operating systems such as Macintosh OSX or Linux.

The first thing to do when using a Microsoft or Macintosh operating system is to purchase virus protection software and update it regularly. Use the program to run periodic scans of your computer for viruses.

It is important to use antivirus software to keep your computer guarded against an attack.

Worms can cause a computer to stop working completely.

Also, since many viruses spread because they have been attached to an executable program, meaning they can't run unless the person opens the program, never open e-mail attachments, files, or programs from an unknown source. By sticking with commercial software, you eliminate almost all the risk from traditional viruses.

Unfortunately, viruses are caused by people who wish to wreak havoc on other people's computer systems and disrupt their lives, and every year

Cybercrime makes victims of unsuspecting computer users.

more of them are released over the Internet. No one can be absolutely certain why someone would choose to create a virus or worm, but it's likely that there will always be people out there working to cause as much trouble as they can. To combat this growing problem, the U.S. and Canadian governments have created legislation that provides stiff fines and jail time for people who spread computer viruses.

In January 2005, Parson was sentenced to eighteen months in prison and and additionally had to perform a hundred hours of community services. He was also expected to spend the first three years after his release under court supervision. Parson got a minimum sentence. He had been facing up to ten years in prison, but the judge said she took into consideration

Fast Fact:
The Original Trojan Horse

In Greek mythology, during the siege of Troy, an enormous wooden horse was left by the Greek army outside the gates of the city. The Greeks then sailed away as if they had retreated. The Trojans, believing the horse to be a religious offering, brought it into the city. That night, Greek soldiers emerged from their hiding place within the hollow horse and opened the city gates to enable the rest of the Greek army to enter and capture Troy.

his age when he released the worm (he was eighteen) and his history of mental illness and family problems.

Unfortunately, many other types of cybercrime are growing in popularity and spreading fast throughout the Internet. As Internet users, we have to remain vigilant in our safety precautions online. Internet scams are on the rise and likely will continue to grow. One of the fastest growing types of cybercrime is called spoofing, and until the government or private businesses figures out how to prevent this type of crime, it is up to us to take safety precautions when we shop online.

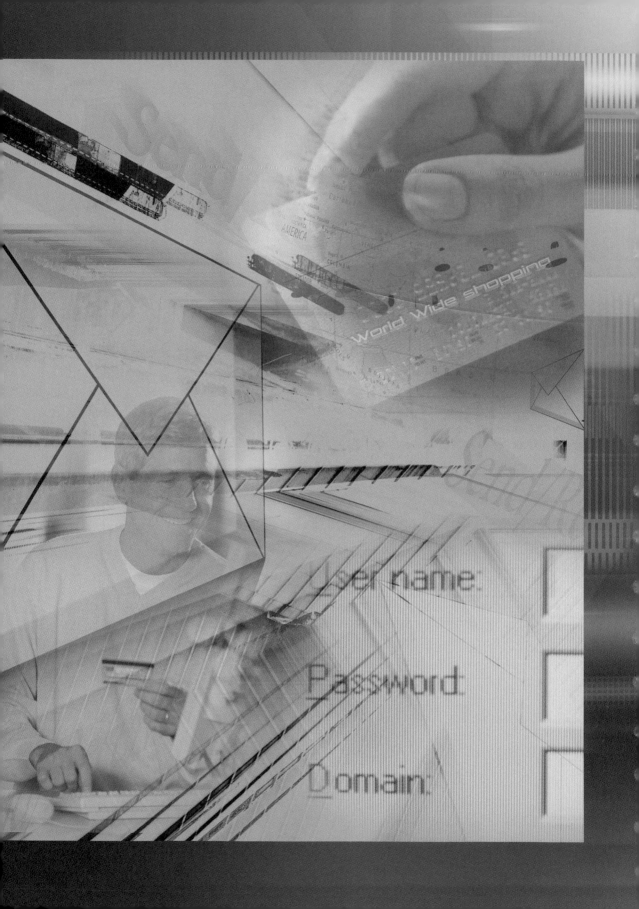

4

Internet
Scams

In April 2004, thousands of e-mail users received urgent messages in their in-boxes. These messages appeared to come from PayPal, and informed recipients that they needed to update their account information. PayPal is a website that allows people to send money to anyone with e-mail. Many people with small online businesses, as well as many people who sell and purchase items through eBay or other online auction sites, use PayPal to send or receive payment through the Internet.

The e-mail instructed users to update their PayPal accounts, and included a link for the user to follow. Once a user followed the link, they could type in their user account names and passwords. The link, however, was not to the real PayPal login site, but to a fake, or "spoofed," PayPal website. When people logged

onto the fake site, they unwittingly gave away their account names and passwords to the creators of the spoofed site.

Spoofing is the practice of creating a fake website that closely mimics a legitimate site in order for the malicious website creator to extract personal information from users of the legitimate site. The creators of the spoofed site send e-mails to trick people into visiting the spoofed site and divulging personal information such as credit card numbers. The act of luring people to the site is called "phishing," which is a hacker term based on the analogy that Internet scammers use e-mail "lures" to "fish" for passwords and financial data from the "sea" of Internet users.

How Spoofing Works

The fake copy of the legitimate website often contains forgeries of many of the clues that help determine a website's authenticity. For example, the malicious user can create a link to the spoofed site that displays the URL of the legitimate website in the status and title bars of the web browser.

In the PayPal example, the spoofed site looked almost exactly like the real PayPal website. It had the same graphics, layout, and wording. Dozens of real PayPal pages were copied and spoofed, including even "Report a Spoof" and "Avoid Fake Websites," so that all the links from the spoofed home page operated and did not leave the site. The fake site even handled registration of new members, with the registration actually going through the real site as well as the spoofed site. In this way, all the data that a new user would enter to join PayPal, including usernames and passwords, could be seen by the creator of the spoofed site. Then the creator could use that data to access the real accounts at PayPal. The spoofed PayPal site had been the most sophisticated one to date. Internet scam artists have gotten very good at phishing and spoofing. For example, earlier spoofed sites were

"Spoofed" websites trick visitors into submitting personal information like their credit card numbers.

more easily spotted than that particular PayPal site. A spoofed Best Buy website did not have e-mails issued from a @bestbuy.com address, but that discrepancy was solved with the PayPal spoof (the e-mail warning people to update their accounts was issued from service@paypal.com).

Other dead giveaways to spoofed sites included sloppy language, spelling mistakes, and bad grammar. Again, all these problems were addressed in the PayPal spoof site; it was extraordinarily complex and a perfect mirror of the original.

Spoofing and Identity Theft

As more and more people use the Internet on a regular basis, some may find spoof websites easier to spot. However, they are still a problem. Recent spoofed websites include Facebook and the U.S. Air Force.

By far, the biggest threat from spoofing is identity theft, when someone steals enough personal information from you—such as your Social Security number, insurance number, credit card numbers, or driver's license number—to impersonate you. With your credit card numbers, people can make purchases online or over the telephone and rack up debt in your name. People can also apply for auto or home loans in your name, and even commit crimes in your name!

Young people are not immune to identity theft. In fact, children are often targets, because the perpetrator usually has many years in which to accumulate debt in a child's name before the child ever applies for a loan. Many teenagers have discovered on applying for a college loan or a car for the first time, that they have a bad credit rating or outstanding debts. Perhaps someone has been using their Social Security or insurance numbers to borrow money and has not paid it back. Unfortunately, even though

Fast Fact

According to a 2011 study, approximately 12 million people in the United States became victims of identity theft in the past year. The increase from previous years may partly be because of the rise in use of smartphones.

victims of identity theft are innocent of the crime, it can take years to clear their names and credit reports.

In the largest identity theft case to date, Philip Cummings, a thirty-five-year-old man, was sentenced to fourteen years in prison for stealing the identities of over 30,000 people across the United States and Canada. From mid-1999 through August 2000, he worked for a software company on Long Island that provided banks and other financial institutions with credit reports. Cummings had access to passwords that allowed him to download virtually any credit report he wanted. He was approached by Nigerian nationals who offered to pay him for copies of credit reports—so he did. Even after leaving the company, his passwords continued to work and he continued to steal and sell credit reports.

Avoiding Spoofed Sites and Phishing Scams

The Anti-Phishing Working Group has compiled a list of resources for how to avoid phishing scams. To help protect yourself online: Be suspicious of any e-mail with urgent requests for personal financial information. Unless the e-mail is digitally signed, you can't be sure it wasn't forged or spoofed. Here are clues to what a phishing scam may look like:

- Phishers typically include upsetting or exciting (but false) statements in their e-mails to get people to react immediately.
- They typically ask for information such as usernames, passwords, credit card numbers, and Social Security numbers.
- Phisher e-mails are typically NOT personalized, while valid messages from your bank or e-commerce company generally are.

Don't use the links in an e-mail to get to any webpage if you suspect the message might not be authentic. Instead, call the company on the telephone, or log onto the website directly by typing the web address into your browser. Avoid filling out forms in e-mail messages that ask for personal financial information. Furthermore, you should only communicate information such as credit card numbers or account information via a secure website or over the telephone. To ensure that you're using a secure website, check the beginning of the URL in your browser address bar. It should be "https://" rather than just "http://."

If you have many online accounts, either through your bank or PayPal, or at any e-commerce sites such as Amazon.com, you should regularly log into your accounts and check your statements to ensure that all transac-

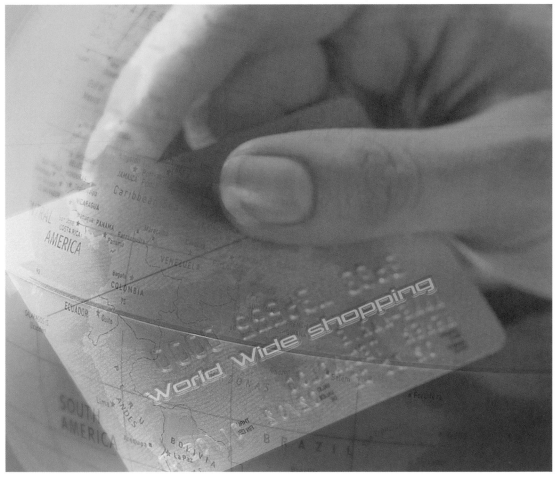

You should only communicate bank or credit card information through a secure website or by telephone.

tions are legitimate. If anything is suspicious, contact your bank or the e-commerce website immediately.

Also, it helps to keep your web browser up to date, and check to see if security patches are applied or needed. For example, people who use Microsoft Internet Explorer can go to the Microsoft Security home page at http://windows.microsoft.com/en-US/windows/security-utilities, and download a special patch relating to certain phishing scams.

Other Internet Scams

There are other types of Internet scams to be aware of too. Internet auction fraud and Nigerian letter fraud are two of the more common ones.

Internet auction fraud is when a seller on an auction site, such as eBay, does not deliver the goods promised, or a purchaser does not pay for the goods that were delivered. This type of fraud accounts for about a quarter of Internet Crimes reported to the FBI.

The Nigerian letter fraud, also called the 419 Fraud, is a scheme that was once done through the postal mail and is now primarily used via e-mail. An e-mail letter is sent that offers the recipient the "opportunity" to share in a percentage of millions of dollars that the author, a self-proclaimed government official, is trying to transfer illegally out of Nigeria. The recipient is encouraged to send information to the author, such as bank names, account numbers, and other identifying information.

The 419 Fraud relies on convincing a willing victim to send money to the author of the letter in several installments of increasing amounts. The letter's author describes in great detail how the money will be spent, all the while promising that all expenses will be returned as soon as the funds are smuggled out of Nigeria. Of course, the alleged millions of dollars do not exist, and the victim eventually ends up with nothing but loss. What's worse, in some cases the perpetrators have taken the bank account information and continued to drain the victim's assets long after the relationship was terminated by the victim.

Although most people with e-mail are now familiar with the 419 hoax, many people fall for it each year. Some people have even been lured to Nigeria, where they were imprisoned. The Nigerian government is very unsympathetic to people who fall for this scheme, because they did, after all, conspire to smuggle funds out of Nigeria in a manner contrary to Nigerian

The 419 Fraud convinces victims to send bank information to supposed government officials in foreign countries.

Internet Scams

Internet scammers may continue to drain your finances as long as they have access to your bank information.

law. The schemes themselves violate section 419 of the Nigerian criminal code, hence the name "419 Fraud."

Tips for Avoiding Internet Scams

The FBI has compiled several lists for avoiding Internet scams.

AVOIDING ONLINE AUCTION FRAUD

- Understand as much as possible about how the auction works, what your obligations are as a buyer, and what the seller's obligations are before you bid.
- Find out what actions the website takes if a problem occurs, and consider insuring the transaction and shipment.
- Learn as much as possible about the seller, especially if the only information you have is an e-mail address.
- Examine the feedback on the seller.
- Determine what method of payment the seller is asking the buyer to use and where he is asking payment to be sent.
- Ask the seller about when delivery can be expected, if the merchandise is covered by warranty, and if it can be exchanged should there be a problem.
- Find out if shipping and delivery are included in the auction price or are added later so there are no unexpected costs.
- There should be no reason to give out your Social Security number, insurance numbers, or driver's license number to the seller.

Online auction sites can enable consumers to find great deals on new or used merchandise, or to find rare and collectible items. However, while most people using online auction sites are legitimate, it pays to be cautious and to follow the tips outlined above.

AVOIDING THE
NIGERIAN LETTER FRAUD

- Be skeptical of individuals representing themselves as Nigerian or other foreign government officials asking for your help in placing large sums of money in overseas bank accounts.
- Do not believe the promise of large sums of money for your cooperation.
- Guard your account information carefully.

The FBI has a tip line for reporting online fraud, scams, and hoaxes. If you need to report this type of activity, go to http://www.ic3.gov and follow the instructions for filling out the form.

The Nigerian letter fraud used to be sent through ground mail, but today it is distributed primarily through e-mail.

Cybercriminals may leave a digital trail that can lead investigators to an arrest.

Overall, it's good to remember that the Internet is a wonderful tool for businesses and consumers alike. It is a reflection of society, however. Just as there will always be criminals in the brick-and-mortar world of commerce, so there will likely be criminals operating in the digital world.

In fact, not only are criminals operating online, but evidence of traditional crimes is often found on the personal and business computers of the people who commit them. In the next two chapters we'll see how computer forensics plays a role in helping to solve crimes not committed on a computer, but leaving digital trails of evidence nonetheless.

5

Corporate Fraud and Computer Evidence

On December 2, 2001, the Houston-based Enron Corporation, one of the world's largest energy trading and communications companies, filed for **Chapter 11 bankruptcy** protection. When this happened, the value of the company's stock plummeted, becoming worthless. Individuals and businesses who had invested money in Enron lost everything they had invested. Furthermore, Enron employees lost their jobs and their retirement savings, and thousands of individuals and hundreds of businesses worldwide that had put money into Enron lost a combined total of billions of dollars. Enron had become the largest business failure in the history of the United States.

Enron was a publicly traded corporation, which means that individuals and businesses could purchase shares of the company, also called stock. Many com-

panies operate this way in order to acquire additional *capital* to invest in new projects. If they were to sell the company, they would lose control over it, so they just sell small parts of it in the form of shares. A large corporation like Enron has thousands of shareholders with some stake in the company. They willingly invest money in the company to help it grow, and in this way the shareholders show a high level of trust in the company.

What was so shocking about Enron's failure was that most people didn't see it coming. Investors had been led to believe that Enron was making money. The value of Enron stock was high, and the business seemed to be performing well. However, for years Enron executives had been falsely reporting profits when in fact they were losing money.

Rules to Protect Investors

Part of what makes publicly traded companies trustworthy is that they must follow certain laws and regulations. For one thing, they must issue a set of documents each year called financial statements, or financial reports. In general, these statements detail how much money the company has earned (its profits) or lost, and how much it has spent. The actual documents are very detailed and include all kinds of information on how the business, as well as any partnerships it is involved in, is faring.

The financial reports must accurately and honestly state how the business is doing financially so investors can make informed decisions about whether to invest in the business. It is illegal and fraudulent for a company to overstate profits in order to acquire new investors or to keep the price of their stocks high. Another law to help prevent fraud requires that the documents be inspected and certified by an independent *auditor*. Enron used one of the five largest accounting firms for this purpose, a company called Arthur Andersen, LLC, of Chicago, Illinois

What Is the Securities and Exchange Commission (SEC)?

The SEC is a U.S. government agency that was established in 1934 to oversee the trading of all issues of securities—which includes shares—by companies offering securities to the public.

Arthur Andersen helped Enron report earnings and profits when they were really losing money and going further into debt. In the fall of 2001, both Enron and Arthur Andersen executives told their employees to shred documents and delete files from their computers in an effort to hide their crimes from the Securities and Exchange Commission (SEC).

Investigations into Arthur Andersen and Enron E-Mails

Since the Enron failure, many of the company's top executives have been arrested and convicted of various crimes, mostly securities fraud. Several top executives at Arthur Andersen have also been convicted of various types of fraud. In fact, the entire Arthur Andersen business was forced to sell most of its assets to other accounting firms because of the Enron scandal. Much of the evidence was captured through email.

While the details of the Enron/Andersen investigation are shrouded in secrecy, computer experts say that what usually happens in such cases is that investigators seize the desktops and laptops of any suspects, as well as mail servers, backup servers, and any other devices that could hold evidence, such as cell phones. With large corporate cases like the one involving Enron and Arthur Andersen, that is no small task, as computer evidence can be widely dispersed around the country, even around the world. But that can be a good thing, too, as in the case of e-mail, where the more widely dispersed the evidence is, the harder it is for anyone to destroy it.

Beginning in early 2002, investigators with the firm Internet Crimes Group in Princeton, New Jersey, began piecing together the case against Arthur Andersen. Arthur Andersen admitted that its auditors for Enron had

To hide any wrongdoing, some corporations shred incriminating documents.

Computer forensic specialists can trace deleted documents that may serve as evidence in a case of securities fraud.

deleted Enron e-mails from October, 23, 2001, until November 9, 2001. Arthur Andersen employees used the e-mail software program Lotus Notes, and case investigators were able to retrieve incriminating e-mail messages that had been deleted up to eight months prior to the start of the investigation. Remember, as mentioned in chapter 1, hitting the delete key only removes the e-mails from the user's view; usually, the data still exists somewhere on the computer hard drive until the computer fills that free space with new data.

Furthermore, e-mails are even harder to delete permanently than other types of data because they often reside in many locations along a computer network. Lotus Notes stores e-mail on a central server and gives most users

The Many Faces of Fraud

In law, fraud is the crime or offense of deliberately deceiving another person, usually in order to unjustly obtain property, money, or services. In criminal law it is called "theft by deception." Fraud can be committed through many methods, including mail, wire, phone, and the Internet. Forms of criminal fraud include:

- Bait and switch, which is a deceptive commercial practice in which customers are induced to visit a store by an advertised sale item and then are told that it is out of stock or that it is far inferior to some more expensive item.

- Confidence tricks, which is a swindle where the victim is defrauded after his or her trust has been won.

- False advertising, which is the crime of publishing, broadcasting, or otherwise publicly distributing an advertisement that contains an untrue, misleading, or deceptive representation or statement knowingly or recklessly made with the intent to promote the sale of property, goods, or services to the public.

- Identity theft, discussed in chapter 4.

- False billing, which is the act of invoicing or otherwise requesting funds from an individual or firm when they don't owe any money.

- Forgery of documents or signatures, which could be signing someone else's name to a check in order to cash it, or creating fake documents in order to make money.

- **Embezzlement**, which is taking money that is under your control, but not yours.

- Health fraud, such as selling products like "quack" medicines, meaning medicines that don't do what the seller claims.

- False insurance claims, which are fraudulent claims filed with an insurance company in order to collect money from them.

- Securities fraud, which includes the practice of deceiving the public about the financial health of a company in order to entice investors to purchase stock in the company.

only limited access, so a person who deletes an e-mail has no way to ensure that it is permanently erased.

Thirty-three defendants were charged in connection with the Enron scandal, including twenty-four former Enron executives. Several were found

Evidence discovered during the Enron investigation has led to the sentencing of Enron executives.

guilty, including Chief Executive Officer Jeffrey Skilling, founder Kenneth Lay, and Chief Financial Officer Andrew Fastow, who pleaded guilty. Skilling was sentenced with twenty-four years in prison, while Lay was given a maximum of forty-five years.

Other Accounting Scandals

In 2002, just after the Enron scandal began unraveling, a wave of accounting scandals rocked the U.S. corporate world. A number of other

Fast Fact

Insider trading is often thought of as an illegal activity, but it is not always so. In one respect, it refers to the legal trading of securities by corporate officers based on information available to the public. But, as in the case of Martha Stewart and Samuel Waksal, it also refers to the illegal trading of securities using privileged information not available to the public.

leading companies have admitted to giving misleading impressions of their financial status. In publicly traded companies like Enron, this type of accounting can amount to fraud, and the SEC has launched a series of investigations.

Other companies under investigation have included: Computer Associates, WorldCom, Tyco, Halliburton, Qwest Communications, Harken Energy, Kmart, Xerox, HealthSouth, and IMClone Systems. IMClone's founder, Samuel Waksal, was convicted of insider trading with his friend Martha Stewart. Stewart was probably the most high-profile corporate executive to go to prison for her crime. She sold her IMClone stock when she knew it was going to fall in price. Some of the key pieces of evidence against her existed on her cell phone and computer, which eventually proved that she had lied to investigators and led to her conviction for obstruction of justice.

Corporate Fraud and Computer Evidence

Corporate crime like the Enron scandal has been going on for as long as corporations have been around. How investigators gather evidence is what's changing. It's no longer just a matter of trying to piece together shredded paper documents; investigators work on piecing together the

Case Study: Is Democracy At Stake?

In the 2004 U.S. presidential election, about three out of ten votes were cast on paperless, direct-recording-electronic (DRE) voting machines. Voters simply touched a computer screen, and the votes were counted on a computer chip embedded in the voting equipment. Unlike receipted transactions at an ATM machine, voters on these machines received no paper record of their vote. And without a paper trail, the votes cannot be recounted or verified if need be.

Doubts about the reliability of computer voting machines have surfaced over the years and continue to surface today. Reports of programming mistakes, software bugs, and computer elections fraud have been in the news for years, but usually only at the local level. Bev Harris, an investigative journalist, put together many stories of computer voting-machine mishaps into one book, published in 2004. Black Box Voting details the many possible malfunctions and security breaches of computer voting machines and the

government officials who sometimes don't want people to know about them. Harris interviewed hundreds of people for the book, including election officials, politicians, computer experts, and even some of the computer programmers who work for the computer voting-machine companies.

In February 2005, Bev Harris, together with computer experts from her website, www.blackboxvoting.org, proved that hacking into a computer voting machine is entirely possible. They hacked into a Diebold computer voting system, in a real location, using the actual setup used on Election Day, November 2, 2004. According to the website, the hack was

> unsophisticated enough that many high school students would be able to achieve it. This hack altered the election by 100,000 votes, leaving no trace at all in the central tabulator program. It did not appear in any audit log. The hack could have been executed in the November 2004 election by just one person.

Harris believes that much needs to be done in the way of election reform, and she's offered her own plan: she thinks each vote should be hand-counted in the presence of observers. Her feeling is that this could be accomplished in a reasonable amount of time through the use of high-speed scanners.

Evidence incriminating Martha Stewart of insider trading was found on her cellular phone.

digital evidence found on hard drives and e-mail servers. And yet, corporate crime is just one of the more "traditional" crimes where digital evidence comes into play. Homicides and child abuse can also leave digital trails of evidence.

6

"Traditional" Crimes Solved with Computer Forensics

On Thursday, December 16, 2004, Bobbie Jo Stinnett, a young woman eight months pregnant with her first child, answered the door of her Kansas home to let in Lisa Montgomery, who had arranged to purchase a rat terrier puppy from Stinnett. Instead, Montgomery strangled Stinnett, cut the fetus from her womb, and kidnapped the premature infant.

Within hours, investigators had a lead on who the killer could have been through information gleaned from Stinnett's computer. Stinnett was a breeder of rat terriers and often frequented a message board for breeders. Another woman who knew Stinnett through the online message board tipped off investigators that Stinnett had posted a message to a woman named Darleen Fischer the night before.

The tip led investigators to search Stinnett's computer for evidence. They were trying to work as quickly as possible, because not only were they looking for the killer, but for the baby, whom they feared might have suffered a loss of oxygen during the mother's strangulation.

Racing against time, investigators checked out who Stinnett had been e-mailing and the Internet sites she had visited. They found she had made plans to sell a puppy to the woman claiming to be Darleen Fischer. When they traced the IP address of Darleen Fischer, it led to the home of Lisa

While investigators still rely on blood and DNA evidence, computers may also hold information important to a case.

A floppy disk led investigators to apprehend a suspect thought to be the serial killer "BTK."

Montgomery, where investigators found her with the baby. Montgomery later confessed to the killing and kidnapping.

Computer Searches in Violent Crimes

Investigators of violent crimes like Stinnett's killing used to ignore the personal computers of the victims in favor of collecting blood, DNA, and fiber and hair samples from the crime scene. Now they realize that computers contain a lot of information about victims' lives. Through computers, investigators can find out who a victim's friends are, who his enemies may be, and the kinds of activities in which he participated. Computers are like a digital diary of many different aspects of our lives and offer many clues about us that can't be ignored in criminal investigations.

In another case, a serial killer had been terrorizing the residents of Wichita, Kansas, since the 1970s; he had murdered ten people, including two children, but had never been found. The killer nicknamed himself BTK, for "bind them, torture them, kill them," and over the years he taunted police by sending them notes, books, and other pieces of evidence daring them to catch him.

The evidence that finally led to an arrest was a computer floppy disk, an older type of data storage. When floppy disks are initialized, the process marks them as unique to a particular computer; as a result, police were able to trace a floppy disk containing evidence back to a computer in a church where Dennis Rader, a sixty-year-old husband and father, volunteered. He was arrested in February 2005, and was sentenced to ten consecutive life terms.

In another homicide case, a forty-year-old woman was brutally murdered, and her former husband became the prime suspect. When investigators seized his home and work computers, they found he had used the Internet to search for phrases that included "how to hire an assassin," "how to kill someone quickly and quietly," and "how to murder someone and not get caught." Although the evidence was controversial—he claimed he was researching crime methods so he could write scripts for the television show *CSI: Crime Scene Investigation*—the evidence was admitted in court. He was found guilty of first-degree murder.

Crimes Against Children

Computers not only offer evidence in traditional crimes, in some cases they help facilitate them. Child abusers have been around forever, but with the **advent** of the Internet, adults who sexually abuse children have found a haven for their way of life in online groups.

According to the FBI, the Internet has become one of the most prevalent techniques used by **pedophiles** to share illegal photographic images of minors and to lure children into illicit sexual relationships. The Internet has dramatically increased the access of sex offenders to the population they seek to victimize. In many of these online groups, adults share photos and video clips of children—including infants, toddlers, and preschool to elementary school-age kids—engaged in sexual activities.

These online groups allow pedophiles the anonymity of the Internet; they don't have to leave their houses to find illegal pornography. Also,

The Internet links communities of pedophiles, making it easier for them to access child pornography.

"Traditional" Crimes Solved
with Computer Forensics

Canadian Laws Regarding Child Pornography

The Canadian Criminal Code defines child pornography as

> a photographic, film, video or other visual representation, whether or not it was made by electronic or mechanical means . . . that shows a person who is or is depicted as being under the age of eighteen years and is engaged in or is depicted as engaged in explicit sexual behavior . . . or the dominant characteristic of which is the depiction, for a sexual purpose, of a sexual organ or the anal region of a person under the age of eighteen years . . . or any written material or visual representation that advocates or counsels sexual activity with a person under the age of eighteen years.

Critics of the law say it leaves too much open for interpretation and that plays such as Romeo and Juliet by William Shakespeare could be banned under the law. As one example, in February 2000, the father of two children in a community near Ottawa was arrested after a technician at a photo lab processed a roll of family snapshots that included four pictures of the man's four-year-old son "goofing around" without his pajama bottoms. Police charged him

with manufacturing child porn. The man was released on bail on condition he leave the family home. The charges were eventually dropped, but the Children's Aid Society demanded a custody hearing and parenting courses for the man and his wife. The man, who had emigrated from Poland, spent his entire savings to clear his name.

Interpreting law is always a tricky business. Lawmakers want to protect children from abuse and also to protect individuals' rights. The Canadian law was updated in 2002 to take into account the Internet, and now makes it a crime to use the Internet to "lure children" into sexual acts or to communicate with them for the purpose of sexual activity.

the online world offers a community of other pedophiles with whom to bond, helping to validate their abuse of children; they can even convince themselves that their activities are normal, since so many other people are involved in the same thing.

Recent arrests have resulted in the confiscation of thousands of computers, hundreds of arrests of pedophiles all over the world, and the discovery of hundreds of thousands of digital images of child sexual abuse. The largest operation to date—Operation Cathedral—involved law enforcement personnel in twelve countries. After a fourteen-month investigation, on September 2, 1998, more than 1,500 officers broke down the doors of suspects in countries around the world, including the United States, Australia, and England. (Forces in Canada pulled out at the last minute.)

"Traditional" Crimes Solved with Computer Forensics

Arrests of child pornographers have turned up thousands of images that were distributed online.

What they discovered shocked the world. Before then, the largest seizure of child pornography had been 7,000 separate images. But the highly organized pedophile ring they busted on that day, called w0nderland (with a zero instead of the letter "o" to help prevent law enforcement from finding it), yielded over 750,000 separate photos and 1,800 digitized video clips of children being sexually abused. A total of 1,236 children appeared in the photos and videos.

Pedophiles use the Internet as a tool to lure young computer users into dangerous situations.

Fighting Online Child Abuse

Online child pornography and child sexual exploitation are the most significant cybercrimes confronting the FBI. To combat this, the FBI has established a task force called the Innocent Images National Initiative (IINI) that specifically targets online pedophiles. The mission of the IINI is threefold: to identify, investigate, and prosecute sexual predators who use the Internet and online services to sexually exploit children; to establish a law enforce-

Images of child pornography may be stored on and shared from a pedophile's computer.

ment presence on the Internet as a deterrent to those who use it to exploit children; and to identify and rescue child victims.

The IINI started during the investigation of the disappearance of a juvenile in May 1993. FBI agents and police in Prince George's County, Maryland, identified two suspects who had sexually exploited numerous juveniles over a twenty-five-year period. Further investigation into the activities of the suspects determined that the adults were routinely utilizing online computers to transmit child pornography.

Investigators soon realized that the utilization of computer telecommunications was rapidly becoming one of the most prevalent techniques by which some sex offenders shared pornographic images of minors and identified and recruited children into sexually illicit relationships. Today, the

IINI focuses on individuals who indicate a willingness to travel between states for the purpose of engaging in sexual activity with a minor, and major producers and/or distributors of child pornography. In addition, the IINI works to identify child victims and obtain appropriate services and assistance for them. The number of cases the IINI addresses annually has risen dramatically over the years, from 113 in 1996 to 2,370 in 2002, to 5,600 pending investigations by April 2012.

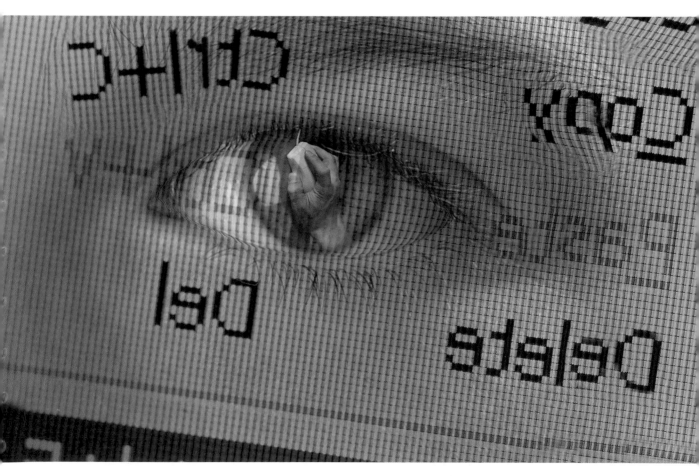

The IINI attempts to investigate and recover children exploited in child pornography.

"Traditional" Crimes Solved
with Computer Forensics

With cybercrime on the rise, digital evidence is an important factor in criminal investigations.

Between cybercrimes like Internet scams and hacking, and traditional crimes like murder and child abuse, digital evidence is on the rise and becoming more important than ever in the courtroom. This means that computer forensic specialists are in high demand.

7

Careers in Computer Forensics

Jason Weiss, a computer forensic technician with the FBI, was trained as a lawyer but then decided that a career with the FBI would be more interesting than working in a law firm. After completing the FBI's rigorous four-month training for special agents, Weiss was assigned to investigative duty in San Diego. A year later, he began working with the computer crime squad.

Weiss has examined hundreds of computers searching for digital evidence of crimes, including various white-collar crimes, international terrorism, crimes against children, and hacking. He also helped the FBI create the San Diego Regional Computer Forensics Laboratory in 1998, which was one of the first computer forensics labs in the United States. Weiss says working for the FBI is "amazing" and adds, "The FBI is the most interesting employer on the planet. You never get bored."

Career opportunities in computer forensics exist in both the public and private sectors.

The need for computer forensic specialists in the workplace is growing.

The FBI recently identified computer crime as one of its top priorities, behind terrorism and counterintelligence. In the United States and Canada, computer crimes such as hacking, fraud, and theft cost consumers and businesses billions of dollars each year. The more we rely on the Internet and e-mail to conduct business and personal affairs, the more criminals will take advantage of it.

Because of this, the need for highly skilled and trained computer forensic technicians is on the rise. Work is available in both the public and the private sectors, and it appears that careers in the field will be booming for quite a while. In the public sector, careers are available in law enforcement at all levels of government, from local municipalities to the FBI, Secret Service, the CIA, and the Department of Homeland Security. In Canada, work as a computer forensic specialist is available at the RCMP. In the private

Fast Fact

In 2010, the RCFL program worked with 130 agencies, conducted 6,564 examinations, and trained 7,403 law enforcement personnel in various digital forensics techniques.

sector, many major corporations now hire their own computer security experts. Although the work differs from law enforcement in how evidence is captured and handled, it embodies many of the same technical skills and knowledge needed to search computers for evidence.

Opportunities in Law Enforcement

The field of computer forensics is growing within government agencies, and along with that, the need for highly skilled computer forensic investigators grows, too. For example, in 2005, the FBI expanded its computer forensic laboratory network. The FBI funds and oversees Regional Computer Forensic Laboratories (RCFLs), which assist any law enforcement agency in their region in cases involving digital evidence, including terrorism, cybercrime, white-collar crime, identity theft, and violent crime. By 2010, there were 16 RCFLs available to almost 7500 law enforcement agents across seventeen states. In all, the program has processed 57,000 hard drives looking for evidence. The RCFL program has bolstered law enforcement efforts in

solving some complex cases, including the murder of Bobbie Jo Stinnett, and assisted in discovering evidence in the BTK serial murder case, as were discussed in the previous chapter.

The FBI isn't the only agency where computer forensic experts will be needed in the coming months and years. According to many experts in the field, opportunities abound across all levels of law enforcement for specialists in computer investigations.

Computer forensic specialists help to piece together the evidence in a crime.

Opportunities abound across all levels of law enforcement for specialists in computer investigations.

However, possessing computer skills and savvy is not enough to work as a computer forensic technician for a law enforcement agency. Background and training in criminal investigations is a key factor in getting hired. This training can come in the form of police officer or special agent training, such as the training Jason Weiss completed when he went to work for the FBI, or it can come from one of the several new programs specially designed to teach computer forensics.

Special Training Programs

Training in computer forensics is now available to professional computer technicians working outside law enforcement. Some organizations that offer certification and training in computer forensics are the International Association of Computer Investigative Specialists and the Southeast Cybercrime Institute.

These training programs offer computer technicians advanced skills in criminal investigations, including evidence handling and how to present technical evidence to a jury. Some computer forensic software vendors also offer training, and a number of universities offer computer forensic programs. For example, the National Center for Forensic Science at the University of Central Florida offers a graduate certificate in the field.

Education Required

Many pathways can lead to a job in computer forensics. As noted earlier, lawyers such as Jason Weiss have entered the field through joining the FBI. Some people simply possess a special talent for computer systems and have the desire to work in law enforcement. Others study computer science for different reasons and then go on to law enforcement training. Still

Some people possess a special talent for computers.

others are law enforcement personnel who have had to acquire training in computers in order to get up to speed with cybercriminals working in the digital age.

It is essential that anyone wishing to work as a computer forensic technician have extensive knowledge of all computer operating systems, including models and systems no longer in use. A degree in computer science is helpful and a great place to start, though it's not necessary if you've entered the law enforcement field through another avenue. As noted al-

While many different paths may lead to a career in computer forensics, all of those paths must include specialized training.

ready, interested law enforcement personnel can acquire special training in computer forensics.

Whether your interest lies in capturing criminals or in the technical challenges of computer searches, a career in computer forensics can be ful-

For some, computer forensics is a fascinating and rewarding career.

filling and very rewarding. As Kevin Gutfleish, an FBI Intelligence Analyst for the IINI, puts it, "I have the unique and important role of protecting kids. And if that isn't enough, I actually get paid to do it every day."

Glossary

advent: The arrival of something important.

auditor: A person authorized to examine and verify financial accounts.

capital: Material wealth in the form of money or property.

Chapter 11 bankruptcy: Bankruptcy laws that govern corporations.

civil: Connected with ordinary citizens and organizations.

concentric: Circles of different sizes with the same middle point.

conspiracy: Joining in a secret agreement to do an unlawful or wrongful act or an act that becomes unlawful as a result of the secret agreement.

corporate fraud: Deliberate deception by a company to obtain money or some other benefit.

e-commerce: Doing business over the Internet or the World Wide Web.

embezzlement: To illegally appropriate property entrusted to one's care to one's own use.

handle: An alias or nickname used on the Internet to maintain anonymity.

latent fingerprints: Fingerprints that remain invisible until treated chemically.

monopolize: To have complete control of an industry or service.

pedophiles: Adults who have sexual desire for children.

restitution: Compensation for a loss, damage, or injury.

wiretap: Device placed on a telephone wire in order to get information.

wrongful termination: Unlawful firing.

Further Reading

Casey, Eoghan. *Handbook of Computer Crime Investigation: Forensic Tools & Technology*. Burlington, Mass.: Academic Press, 2001.

Casey, Eoghan. *Digital Evidence and Computer Crime*. Burlington, Mass.: Academic Press, 2004.

Farmer, Dan, and Wietse Venema. *Forensic Discovery*. Boston, Mass.: Addison Wesley Professional, 2004.

McClure, Stuart, Joel Scambray, and George Kurtz. *Hacking Exposed: Network Security Secrets & Solutions*. Emeryville, Calif.: McGraw-Hill Osborne Media, 2003.

Nelson, Bill. *Computer Forensics and Investigations*. Boston, Mass.: Muska & Lipman, 2004.

Phillips, Amelia. *Guide to Computer Forensics and Investigation*. Boston, Mass.: Course Technology, 2003.

Schweitzer, Douglas. *Computer Forensics: Incident Response Essentials*. Emeryville, Calif.: McGraw-Hill Osborne Media, 2003.

Verton, Dan. *The Hacker Diaries: Confessions of Teenage Hackers*. Berkeley, Calif.: McGraw-Hill, 2002.

For More Information

American Academy of Forensic Sciences
www.aafs.org

Black Box Voting
www.blackboxvoting.org

Computer Crime Research Center
www.crime-research.org

Computer Training Schools
www.computertrainingschools.com/?googlesecurity=y&got=computer_forensics&t=160

Cybercrime
www.justice.gov/criminal/cybercrime

Hacking Sites
www.technology-resource.co.uk/hacking.asp

International Association of Computer Investigative Specialists
www.cops.org

FBI
www.fbi.gov

Regional Computer Forensic Laboratory
www.rcfl.gov

Publisher's note:
The websites listed on this page were active at the time of publication. The publisher is not responsible for websites that have changed their addresses or discontinued operation since the date of publication. The publisher will review and update the website list upon each reprint

Index

BTK killer 86, 101

Canadian laws regarding child pornography 88–89
careers in computer forensics 97–106
computer forensic specialists 10–11, 13–15, 17–18
computer forensic technology 21–23
computer forensics, defined 10
    uses 10–12
computers
    how they work 16, 18–19
corporate fraud 69–81
    Arthur Andersen 70–73
    Enron 69–73, 75–78
crimes against children 86–93, 95

hacking 25–43
    "black hat" hackers 32, 33
    Mafiaboy 26–27, 29, 31–32, 33, 35, 39–42
    "white hat" hackers 31–32

Innocent Images National Initiative (IINI) 91–93, 106
Internet networks 28–29

Internet scams 55–67
    auction fraud 62, 65
    Nigerian letter fraud 62, 64, 66
    phishing 56, 60–61
    spoofing 53, 56, 58

Microsoft 9–10, 13, 45, 50, 61
Mitnick, Kevin 36–37

Parson, Jeffrey Lee 45–46, 49, 52–53

Regional Computer Forensic Laboratories (RCFL) 97, 100

Securities and Exchange Commission (SEC) 71
Stinnett, Bobbie Jo 83–84

traditional crimes 67, 83–95
Trojan horses 46, 49, 53

virus 43, 46–47, 49–52
virus protection 50–53

worms 43, 45–46, 47, 49, 50, 52
    Code Red worm 48–49

Picture Credits

Comstock: pp. 63, 103, 104

Dreamstime.com:
  Cammeraydave: p. 80
  Ilja Mašík: p. 98
  Olivier Le Queinec: p. 22

Photos.com: pp. 12, 15, 17, 21, 30, 31, 34, 38, 40, 41, 42, 50, 51, 52, 57, 61, 64, 66, 67, 72, 73, 76, 84, 85, 87, 90, 91, 92, 93, 95, 98, 99, 101, 105, 106

To the best knowledge of the publisher, all other images are in the public domain. If any image has been inadvertently uncredited, please notify Vestal Creative Services, Vestal, New York 13850, so that rectification can be made for future printings.

Biographies

AUTHOR

Elizabeth Bauchner lives in Ithaca, New York. A lifelong "health nut," Elizabeth enjoys bicycling, hiking, and swimming with her children. She writes about healthy vegetarian food and nutrition for ChefMom.com, as well as the *Ithaca Journal*. She's also written many articles on women's and children's health issues for consumer and trade publications.

SERIES CONSULTANTS

Carla Miller Noziglia is Senior Forensic Advisor for the U.S. Department of Justice, International Criminal Investigative Training Assistant Program. A Fellow of the American Academy of Forensic Sciences, Ms. Noziglia served as chair of the board of Trustees of the Forensic Science Foundation. Her work has earned her many honors and commendations, including Distinguished Fellow from the American Academy of Forensic Sciences (2003) and the Paul L. Kirk Award from the American Academy of Forensic Sciences Criminalistics Section. Ms. Noziglia's publications include *The Real Crime Lab* (coeditor, 2005), *So You Want to be a Forensic Scientist* (coeditor, 2003), and contributions to *Drug Facilitated Sexual Assault* (2001), *Convicted by Juries, Exonerated by Science: Case Studies in the Use of DNA* (1996), and the *Journal of Police Science* (1989). She is on the editorial board of the *Journal for Forensic Identification*.

Jay Siegel is Director of the Forensic and Investigative Sciences Program at Indiana University-Purdue University, Indianapolis and Chair of the Department of Chemistry and Chemical Biology. He holds a Ph.D. in Analytical Chemistry from George Washington University. He worked for three years at the Virginia Bureau of Forensic Sciences, analyzing drugs, fire residues, and trace evidence. From 1980 to 2004 he was professor of forensic chemistry and director of the forensic science program at Michigan State University in the School of Criminal Justice. Dr. Siegel has testified over 200 times as an expert witness in twelve states, Federal Court and Military Court. He is editor in chief of the *Encyclopedia of Forensic Sciences*, author of *Forensic Science: A Beginner's Guide and Fundamentals of Forensic Science*, and he has more than thirty publications in forensic science journals. Dr. Siegel was awarded the 2005 Paul Kirk Award for lifetime achievement in forensic science. In February 2009, he was named Distinguished Fellow by the American Academy of Forensic Sciences.